Why Cancer Is Not Bad Luck

*Finding comfort, grace, and salvation
through the love of Jesus Christ*

Ronald D. Daves

WESTBOW
PRESS
A DIVISION OF THOMAS NELSON

Unless otherwise indicated, biblical references are from the New King James Version.

WestBow Press books may be ordered through booksellers or by contacting:

WestBow Press
A Division of Thomas Nelson
1663 Liberty Drive
Bloomington, IN 47403
www.westbowpress.com
1-(866) 928-1240

Because of the dynamic nature of the Internet, any web addresses or links contained in this book may have changed since publication and may no longer be valid. The views expressed in this work are solely those of the author and do not necessarily reflect the views of the publisher, and the publisher hereby disclaims any responsibility for them.

Any people depicted in stock imagery provided by Thinkstock are models, and such images are being used for illustrative purposes only.
Certain stock imagery © Thinkstock.

ISBN: 978-1-4497-5724-3 (sc)
ISBN: 978-1-4497-5725-0 (e)

Library of Congress Control Number: 2012911279

Printed in the United States of America

WestBow Press rev. date: 6/26/2012

To Karen my wonderful wife,
editor, proofreader, and compiler of this work.

To the faithful people of God who are dealing with the news of cancer or the news of an illness unto death that comes to all humanity; to those who desire to live out that news through the grace of God, having in mind the glory of God and the redemption of the lost around them for the Kingdom of God.

May this book be a source of great comfort in God's promises. May my Father in heaven grant you the comfort He has given me in my time of dealing with cancer.

May this book bring those that do not know and have not come to believe in the Lord Jesus Christ as Savior, not only the comfort of God in Christ, but bring them to confession and belief in Christ to salvation and everlasting life.

Contents

Acknowledgments

I would like to thank and acknowledge those who have helped me in putting these thoughts together.

First, to the Lord Jesus Christ who has saved me and has been faithful to not forsake me. To the powerful and living word of God which brings encouragement and comfort in times of need.

I also want to thank the many people of Temple Baptist Church for their support both in spiritual and physical ways. To Karen's previous employer Shandon United Methodist Church for their prayers and many expressions of support and help. To our daughter's church Varennes Heights Baptist Church for their continued prayers and support. To our friends that have prayed and continue to pray . . . I say thank you to all.

Special thanks to my sweet Karen who has been with me throughout this whole process. Before, during and after the news, the tests and procedures, she has been the most wonderful helpmeet, spiritual counselor and comforter just as 2 Corinthians promises. To our daughter Sandi and husband Weldon, our son Ronnie and wife Brandi, and to my six grandsons; Andrew, Aaron, Alex, Adam; Logan and Landon.

May God receive the glory and we receive His very best.

Introduction

This book is my attempt to share with you the great comfort of God's grace that I have found in dealing with the news of cancer, illness or death. Paul speaks of this truth in 2 Corinthians 1:3-5 *"Blessed be the God and Father of our Lord Jesus Christ, the Father of mercies and God of all comfort, who comforts us in all our tribulation, that we may be able to comfort those who are in any trouble, with the comfort with which we ourselves are comforted by God. For as the sufferings of Christ abound in us, so our consolation also abounds through Christ."*

Paul tells us God is the God of comfort and mercy through all tribulations and He gives that same comfort and mercy to His own (see chapter three on how to become a child of God). Comfort and mercy are given that we may share the comfort and mercy of God with others in need. This is my goal and intent through this book. I want to share with you the comfort and mercy God has extended to me as I deal with the news of cancer in my own life.

We come to a topic like cancer, sickness, suffering and death and even though we know it is true and real it is the last thing that anyone ever wants to speak about. We know the truth of our mortality hangs over us every day. Somehow in the busyness of our lives we either ignore our mortality or don't give it a thought. But the day our bodies stop or a doctor tells us we have cancer and our bodies waste away or hurt; we are reminded we have the same terminal illness, we will all die.

I hope this book will be a great comfort to you who know the Lord Jesus and a great comfort for you who do not. To those who know the Lord Jesus His grace and comfort will be great to you through it all. For those that do not, you can come to know the Lord and His grace will be great to you as well. God has not left us in the dark without hope and help. The Bible, God's holy word has been given to us to meet our every need. The Bible has no errors and is perfect. It is God's word to us to know Him and His love for us.

Therefore, I want to share several Scriptures before we start.

Romans 8:28 "And we know that all things work together for good to those who love God, to those who are the called according to His purpose."

Jeremiah 1:5 "Before I formed you in the womb I knew you; Before you were born I sanctified you; I ordained you a prophet to the nations."

Isaiah 43:1-3 "But now, thus says the LORD, who created you, O Jacob, And He who formed you, O Israel: "Fear not, for I have redeemed you; I have called you by your name; You are Mine. When you pass through the waters, I will be with you; And through the rivers, they shall not overflow you. When you walk through the fire, you shall not be burned, Nor shall the flame scorch you. For I am the LORD your God, The Holy One of Israel, your Savior."

Romans 8:1 "There is therefore now no condemnation to those who are in Christ Jesus, who do not walk according to the flesh, but according to the Spirit."

Ecclesiastes 3:2 "A time to be born, And a time to die."

Psalm 116:15 "Precious in the sight of the LORD is the death of His saints."

We see in God's holy word all the wonderful thoughts God thinks in regard to us and has given to us. He works all things out for good to us who know Him, He created us the very person He desires us to be, He has prepared a way for us to be saved and have all condemnation removed and tells us there is a time for us to be born and a time for us to die.

Chapter One

Why Cancer is Not Bad Luck

I would like to share with you the background of why I titled this book, *Why Cancer Is Not Bad Luck.*

I am a pastor and in November 2011, I resigned my present church to move on to a new ministry position. I was tired during that time but credited it to stress or weariness dealing with a move. In the transition period between resigning my church and starting a new ministry I was diagnosed with cancer. Therefore, I found myself without a ministry position and facing cancer.

I picked my wife up from her work on Thursday, November 10 and she noticed that I was jaundice. We immediately went to our local Doctor's Care. There they drew blood thinking I had hepatitis. They called Friday night letting me know I did not have hepatitis and set up an appointment for a CT scan on Tuesday. Following the CT scan they referred me to a gastroenterologist. On Wednesday I went to the gastroenterologist who told me I had cancer. I have a Klatskin tumor in the bile duct of my liver. At the time he did not know if it was operable.

As I sat in the doctor's office after he told me I had cancer, that it would take a major surgery to remove it, and only if it was removable, I was stunned to say the least. I asked him a question of how did this occur. Why did I get this kind of the cancer? I wondered if there was something that I had eaten over the years or something I had been exposed to that caused a cancer like this. He simply stated it was "bad luck". At first I may have agreed or felt like it was bad luck, but to those of us who know the Lord Jesus Christ there is no such thing as bad luck. There is no such thing as bad luck even though this was bad news.

Why do I say that? Because God is the creator of all things, He watches over all things, and brings all things to pass under His good, careful and watchful eye. Nothing takes Him by surprise.

In the Old Testament Isaiah 46:10 says this about God; *"Declaring the end from the beginning, And from ancient times things that are not yet done, Saying, 'My counsel shall stand, And I will do all My pleasure.'"* God is the Creator of all things. He is the sustainer of all things and He accomplishes and performs all things that He desires. All things are under God's control and are always good. This verse tells me this bad news delivered by the doctor my God from ancient times not only knew about but by the good counsel of His will has allowed.

The New Testament also declares this same thought about God and His wonderful control of all things. It says in Ephesians 1:11, *"In Him also we have obtained an inheritance, being predestined according to the purpose of Him who works all things according to the counsel of His will."* This verse tells us that God by His own infinite wisdom and according to the counsel of His will, performs all things He so desires. This means everything that occurs around us, and to us, is from the almighty hand of a loving God, who is working out His perfect counsel.

Jesus reveals this same truth in Matthew 10:29 *"Are not two sparrows sold for a copper coin? And not one of them falls to the ground apart from your Father's will."* Jesus tells us that not a sparrow, one of the smallest and insignificant animals on earth, can fall to the ground without God knowing it. Then Jesus reveals to us that we are of more value than these sparrows, *"Do not fear therefore; you are of more value than many sparrows."* (Matthew 10:31)

We come to times like these in which we receive news of cancer or sickness and are tempted to think it is just bad luck. The words luck, chance or fate are only words. There is no such thing as luck, good or bad. There is no such thing as chance, good or bad. There is no such thing as fate, good or bad. Yet, every day we see people who receive bad news or good news or any news and credit it to luck, chance, or fate.

Thinking the bad news we have received is bad luck will cause us to turn inward, to start questioning why, for which there is no answer. When we do not believe in the God who has created all things, rules all things by the good counsel of His will, and we attribute what is happening to us as luck, we have no hope or help, which can quickly lead to despair. Turning to and looking to God our Creator and knowing that He rules and reigns according to the good counsel of His will leads us to the place of receiving the comfort that God indeed wants to comfort us with.

It is not easy to receive the news of cancer or any other sickness or disease. When we know God is ruling and reigning and that He is good and we are under and in that great good care of the one true God, this gives us hope. Hope because it is a good, wise, great, creator God who allows our lives to be under the counsel of His will.

Cancer is not bad luck even though it is bad news. It is alright to accept the news of your cancer as bad news but not as bad luck. Turn away from luck and turn to the Lord God, who is the rewarder of those that seek Him (Hebrews 11:6).

Chapter Two

Why Cancer is Possibly a Chariot

In this chapter I want to deal with a topic the entire world knows is true. That topic is death. Even Alex Trebek reminds us of this truth in his television commercial on life insurance. Alex Trebek seeks to sells us life insurance policies for our funeral and final expenses. Even when we know death is a reality we try not think about it. Because it is true and because God cares for us and rules all things according to the counsel of His will He desires for us not only to think about it but turn to Him.

In the Old Testament 2 Kings 2 deals with the death of Elijah, the prophet of God. Elisha was going to replace Elijah as the prophet of God. When the time came for Elijah to die, Elisha was with him and asked for a double portion of the power of God to be upon him. Elijah told Elisha in 2 Kings 2:10-11 *"You have asked a hard thing. Nevertheless, if you see me when I am taken from you, it shall be so for you; but if not, it shall not be so." Then it happened, as they continued and talked, that suddenly a chariot of fire appeared with horses of fire, and separated the two of them; and Elijah went up by a whirlwind into heaven."* Indeed following this

Elisha did receive a double portion as he saw Elijah go to heaven in a chariot.

We see that Elijah knew that he was going to die or be taken up even though he did not know the mode of transportation that would take him. The same is true for us. We know we are going to die someday but we do not know the mode or the way it will occur.

Knowing that we are all going to die should lead us to prepare for that death. We probably will not go to heaven by a chariot of fire as Elijah did but we will be transported one way or the other. It may be cancer or some other sickness or disease. We will all have a chariot of some type of transport that carries us out of this life, the process we call death.

The Bible tells us in 1 Corinthians 15:53-54 *"For this corruptible must put on incorruption, and this mortal must put on immortality. So when this corruptible has put on incorruption, and this mortal has put on immortality, then shall be brought to pass the saying that is written: "Death is swallowed up in victory."* We are all mortal and this mortality one day will be replaced with immortality. So when we hear the news of our cancer or sickness knowing it is within the good wise counsel of God, for some it may be the very chariot that God uses to transport us to Himself. For those who know the Lord Jesus Christ and believe in God this is not a bad thought but a comforting thought knowing our mortality must be replaced with immortality for us to be transported into the presence of God.

We will all die, it says in Ecclesiastes 3:2 *"A time to be born, And a time to die."* We have kept the appointment to be born, and someday we will keep the appointment of death. No one knows what our mode of transportation will be for transport out of this world.

Chapter Three

Why Cancer is to Bring Us to Faith

Death is a reality and we know we will die; yet humanity was not created to die. Dying is foreign to humanity even though we know everyone dies. In a real sense we do not know how to die. We were not created to die but were created by God to know Him and enjoy Him forever.

In the beginning when God created Adam and Eve they were created to know God, walk with God and enjoy not only God but all of God's creation. This is still the desire of God for you and me that we would come to know Him and enjoy Him. Death came as a result of or because of sin.

God told Adam and Eve the day they ate of the fruit that He prohibited, they would die. God was telling them to enjoy Him through obedience and faith and they would live and enjoy Him and all of creation forever, never to die. But if and when they disobeyed they would die. God told Adam this truth in Genesis 2:17 *"but of the tree of the knowledge of good and evil you shall not eat, for in the day that you eat of it you shall surely die."*

Adam and Eve disobeyed God and ate of the fruit that He prohibited. God told Adam after they disobeyed him in Genesis 3:19 this truth; *"In the sweat of your face you shall eat bread till you return to the ground, For out of it you were taken; For dust you are, And to dust you shall return."*

Adam and Eve from the day they disobeyed God no longer enjoyed fellowship with the Lord each day. They no longer enjoyed fellowship with each other from that day, and Adam and Eve would see their son Cain kill their son Abel. Adam and Eve disobeyed God and this disobedience is called sin. This sin caused the separation between them and God; between each other and all humanity. This same sin is what brings death and finds us in need of God's restoration and salvation.

The Bible is clear about the sin of Adam and how it has corrupted the whole human race, including you and me. The Bible reveals in Romans 5:12 this corruption to mankind, *"Therefore, just as through one man sin entered the world, and death through sin, and thus death spread to all men, because all sinned."* This one-man, meaning Adam, is how sin entered the world and how death entered the world and how this sin and death spread to all of us. We know this sin spread to all of us for the Bible tells us in Romans 3:23 *"for all have sinned and fall short of the glory of God."* Romans 6:23 tells us of the penalty for this sin. *"For the wages of sin is death, but the gift of God is eternal life in Christ Jesus our Lord."* This verse makes it clear if one sins, the wages one receives is death. The Bible is true and very clear that death comes upon all who have sinned as a wage for that sin, Adam died, Eve died, Cain, Abel, and every human being from that time to the end of history will die because they are sinners and have sinned.

The Bible makes it clear God is not pleased with the death of anyone. Ezekiel 33:11 says, *"Say to them: 'As I live,' says the Lord GOD, 'I have no pleasure in the death of the wicked, but that the wicked turn from his way and live. Turn, turn from your evil ways! For why should you die, O house of Israel?'"* God is not pleased with the death of anyone, meaning separation from Him, not knowing Him or enjoying Him forever. Death is one of the means by which God allows us to recognize our need of Him, our need of turning to Him, by faith believing and trusting in Him. Even though we may be facing cancer or some other sickness God is not concerned with just our death but desires it to be the means by which we would turn to Him in faith, trusting Him, knowing that His perfect and good counsel is best for us.

The Bible tells us in II Peter 3:9 the desire of the Lord is that none perish; *"The Lord is not slack concerning His promise, as some count slackness, but is longsuffering toward us, not willing that any should perish but that all should come to repentance."* God is not willing that we die and perish but that we come to repentance. The word repentance means to say the same thing, to think the same thing, or to agree with. What is it that God wants us to agree with Him about? God desires that we agree with Him that we have disobeyed and sinned against Him, understanding we will die and be separated from Him if we do not repent.

The Bible tells us in John 3:16 *"For God so loved the world that He gave His only begotten Son, that whoever believes in Him should not perish but have everlasting life."* Indeed God so loved us that He sent His only son, the Lord Jesus Christ, who came to die on the cross for our sin. If we will believe God and repent of our sin, we will not perish but have everlasting life. The Bible tells us in Romans 10:9-10 how to receive this repentance and faith, *"that if you confess with your mouth the Lord Jesus and believe in your heart that God has raised Him from the dead, you will be saved. For with the heart one believes unto righteousness, and with the mouth confession is made unto salvation."* For us to be saved, to have the salvation of the Lord, we must believe and confess and the Lord will save us. We will not perish, but everlasting life will be ours through the finished work of Jesus Christ our Lord.

Our cancer makes us stop and assess our life in light of eternal things. My prayer is that it will help us to look toward God, through the Lord Jesus Christ, by the power the Holy Spirit believing Him unto everlasting life.

Chapter Four

Why Cancer is an Example to Follow

When it comes to cancer or any other sickness we begin to think no one else has traveled this path before. But in truth we know that is not the case. Many have gone on before just as we may find ourselves today. We have a body that is growing old and even if disease never attacks our body, we would still grow old and die. We live in a world that is decaying because of the sin that Adam brought into this world, and that decay is seen in our lives and our bodies day by day.

We seek release from this decaying earth and decaying body yet Christ entered this world to take on Himself the very things we seek release from. Christ was in heaven with no sin, no death, no decay and came to this earth to die for us. We who are on the earth in suffering and pain are seeking heaven and comfort. Christ who had heaven and comfort came to this earth to suffer and die for our salvation. Jesus Christ truly suffered for all who will believe.

The Bible tells us in John 3:16 *"For God so loved the world that He gave His only begotten Son, that whoever believes in Him should not perish but have everlasting life."* The example that Christ gives us in this verse is that He left heaven and gave Himself to suffering and death that we might believe Him and not perish. Jesus told his disciples the same thing in John 3:13 *"No one has ascended to heaven but He who came down from heaven, that is, the Son of Man who is in heaven."* Jesus states in John 6:51 *"I am the living bread which came down from heaven. If anyone eats of this bread, he will live forever; and the bread that I shall give is My flesh, which I shall give for the life of the world."* Jesus the son of the living God, God of very God, who was in heaven without suffering or pain or death, left heaven and came down to earth so we who are suffering and dying may be able to turn and believe on Him and not perish.

The Bible also tells us in Hebrews 4:14-15 *"Seeing then that we have a great High Priest who has passed through the heavens, Jesus the Son of God, let us hold fast our confession. For we do not have a High Priest who cannot sympathize with our weaknesses, but was in all points tempted as we are, yet without sin."* Jesus having come to this earth has suffered in every point that we as humans have suffered yet without sin, that He might save us and give us an example of how we also could suffer for His glory. That is why the Bible tells us in Hebrews 12:2 *"looking unto Jesus, the author and finisher of our faith, who for the joy that was set before Him endured the cross, despising the shame, and has sat down at the right hand of the throne of God."* Why did Jesus come to this earth and suffer and die on the cross? So we even in our suffering here on this earth would be able to look onto Him and suffer as He did with the same joy knowing that believing in God we will not be abandoned or forsaken.

As believers knowing that our salvation is sure and our home in heaven is secure in Christ we also can suffer following the example of Jesus our Savior. It is not easy and sometimes most difficult but we can trust, turn and believe that even in our suffering we know God is going to bring all too good. Peter tells us in 1 Peter 2:21 *"For to this you were called, because Christ also suffered for us, leaving us an example, that you should follow His steps."* Peter was writing to first century Christians who were suffering persecution for their faith. They would lose their homes, their jobs, they would be outcast and many of them would die because they were believers. Peter told them that they were called unto this for the glory of the Lord, the encouragement of the Saints, and the salvation of those lost in the community.

For us to be able to do this same thing we have to follow after humility. That is what we find in Philippians 2:8 *"And being found in appearance as a man, He humbled Himself and became obedient to the point of death, even the death of the cross."* We see that Jesus humbled Himself even to the point of death on the cross to be obedient to God and to bring salvation to us. We must also humble ourselves even to the point of death for the glory of the Lord. The apostle Paul, one of the great saints of the New Testament era, strove for this humility as an example of suffering. Paul states in Philippians 3:10-11 *"that I may know Him and the power of His resurrection, and the fellowship of His sufferings, being conformed to His death, if, by any means, I may attain to the resurrection from the dead."* Paul wanted to know the Lord Jesus in a powerful way. Paul understood knowing Christ comes by the fellowship of his suffering, even being conformed to Christ's death. Paul knew through suffering he would understand how wonderful, and privileged one is to believe they have salvation through Christ.

Job, of the Old Testament, shows us this same humility and passion to know the Lord and to trust the Lord even to the point of death. Job 2:10 says, *"But he said to her, "You speak as one of the foolish women speaks. Shall we indeed accept good from God, and shall we not accept adversity?"* Job was saying can we only accept, receive, and expect from God good always and that good being only what we believe is good? No, Job says we can trust God to give us good even in what we perceive is bad news. We can trust God and know all things can work towards good in the life of the believer. Listen to what Job says in Job 13:15 *"Though He slay me, yet will I trust Him."* Job was saying God is so good that even if He takes my life I will continue to believe, trust, and obey Him.

The Old Testament prophet Habakkuk says the same thing in Habakkuk 3:17-19 *"Though the fig tree may not blossom, Nor fruit be on the vines; Though the labor of the olive may fail, And the fields yield no food; Though the flock may be cut off from the fold, And there be no herd in the stalls -- Yet I will rejoice in the LORD, I will joy in the God of my salvation. The LORD God is my strength; He will make my feet like deer's feet, And He will make me walk on my high hills."* The prophet Habakkuk was saying indeed we receive all the good things from the Lord and if they stop, yet will we rejoice, yet will our joy be in the God who we have trusted and believed. What do Peter, Paul, Job, and Habakkuk have? They have faith in the living God, trusting in His good, sovereign will, and in the example Christ set by leaving heaven.

When thinking upon the suffering of Christ, the perfect son of the living God who was without sin, we must be reminded that He did not do this for any other reason except the glory of the Father in heaven and the salvation of those who believe upon Him. The suffering that Christ experienced and underwent was truly suffering and pain that brought real death to Him. He died so that we might live. He suffered that we might know that we could suffer for and with Him. We know that ultimately our suffering will bring us to the end of our life, to that eternal life that God has promised to all who will believe in the Lord Jesus Christ.

In John MacArthur's book *Anxiety Attacked* this prayer
is attributed to Thomas A. Kempis.
"O Lord . . . greater is Thy anxiety for me (Matt. 6:30;
John 6:20),
than all the care that I can take for myself.
For he standeth but very totteringly, who casteth not all
his anxiety upon Thee (1 Peter 5:7).
O Lord, if only my will may remain right and firm
towards Thee,
do with me whatsoever it shall please Thee.
For it cannot be anything but good,
whatsoever Thou shalt do with me.
If Thou willest me to be in darkness, be Thou blessed;
and if Thou willest me to be in light,
be Thou again blessed.
If Thou vouchsafe to comfort me, be Thou blessed;
and if Thou willest me to be afflicted,
be Thou ever equally blessed."
(revised translation by Geoffrey Cumberlege, Oxford
University Press, n.d.).
MacArthur, John F., Jr. *Anxiety Attacked* (Wheaton,
Illinois: Victor Books, 1996, c 1993), 52.

May this be our prayer that not only would we follow the example
of Jesus in suffering but with joy we would ask the Lord to help
us to do it for His glory.

Chapter Five

Why Cancer is a Time of Reflection

After the sudden shock of the news of cancer and time of processing it, we must allow our cancer to bring us to a time of spiritual reflection. This spiritual reflection should bring us to a time of repenting and rejoicing. Not everyone will be given this time, yet we who have been given the news of cancer often have just such a period of time. This time of reflection is to continue our seeking to be pure in heart before the Lord Jesus who has saved and empowered us to do so. Rejoice that you have time to come before the Lord seeking purity of heart. The Bible tells us the pure in heart will see God in Matthew 5:8 *"Blessed are the pure in heart, For they shall see God."* We need to use our time to come before the Lord and His Word in a purity of heart.

In Chapter 10 of his book, *Don't Waste Your Cancer,* John Piper states *"Are our besetting sins as attractive to us now as they were before we had cancer? If so we are wasting our cancer. Cancer is designed to destroy the appetite for sin. Pride, greed, lust, hatred, unforgiveness, impatience, laziness, procrastination —all these are adversaries that cancer is meant to attack. Don't just think of battling against cancer.*

Also think of battling with cancer." Piper, John, *Don't Waste Your Cancer (Wheaton, Illinois: Crossway, 2011)* 23.

The apostle Paul in Romans 7:13-25 shares the conflict he had in this life. He wanted to do all for the glory of the Lord. He states in this passage the things that he wanted to do he could not do and the things that he did not want to do were the very things that he did. Revealing to us that this is the same battle everyone should fight and reflect on to arrive at a purity of heart. Paul tells us in 2 Corinthians 12:7 *"and lest I should be exalted above measure by the abundance of the revelations, a thorn in the flesh was given to me, a messenger of Satan to buffet me, lest I be exalted above measure."* I believe Paul was saying the Lord allowed his body to be given a thorn so he would do battle with sin and strive towards purity of heart. I'm not saying that Paul's thorn was cancer but I am saying that it was a thorn in his flesh that caused him to battle with sin.

I believe the battle with sin can be won as we reflect on sin under God's love and our standing in God's love.

Reflecting upon our sin and God's love allows us to see that God loved us while we were still sinners. That He removed all condemnation from our life placing that condemnation on Christ Jesus our Lord who paid the penalty for sin. The Bible tells us in Romans 5:8 *"But God demonstrates His own love toward us, in that while we were still sinners, Christ died for us."* This verse tells us that while we were sinning Christ died for us, He did not wait for us to become good or to do something good before He would accept us. The Bible says in Romans 8:1 *"There is therefore now no condemnation to those who are in Christ Jesus, who do not walk according to the flesh, but according to the Spirit."* This verse tells us there is no condemnation on us that have come to believe and trust in the Lord Jesus Christ. God's love provided through Christ was offered to us while we were sinners and is offered to us when we come to believe on the Lord Jesus Christ bringing to us complete forgiveness with no condemnation.

Reflecting on God's love allows us to see four different elements of God's love given to us through Christ. Reflecting on these will allow us to do battle with sin during our time of cancer. Because God loves us, we stand in His love, His goodness, His authority, and His presence.

Reflect on our standing in God's love. God loves us so greatly that while we were sinners He died for us. Having died for us we can believe in the Lord Jesus Christ for the forgiveness of our sin and the salvation of our soul and the removal of all condemnation. If that were not enough the Bible tells us in Romans 8:35 *"Who shall separate us from the love of Christ? Shall tribulation, or distress, or persecution, or famine, or nakedness, or peril, or sword?"* This verse tells us that nothing will ever separate us from the love of God; His love is so great that even our cancer will not separate us from His love. So during this time of our cancer let us stand in God's love for He truly loves us.

Reflect on our standing in God's goodness. It is important for us to understand God's goodness. God is good and everything that He allows is good and right. We may not see it, understand it, or even like it but because He is good, He always does what is good and right. Reflecting on this will allow us to hold onto the goodness of God we stand in. Jesus tells us in Matthew 19:17 when speaking to one who was questioning him, *"So He said to him, "Why do you call Me good? No one is good but One, that is, God."* Because God is good that leads us to the passage of Scripture that we find in Romans 8:28 *"And we know that all things work together for good to those who love God, to those who are the called according to His purpose."* We who come to know that God is good, and believe and trust in Him, know that all things do indeed work together for good because God is good. I may not feel it, understand it, or even like it today as I reflect on my cancer but reflecting on my standing in God's goodness I know ultimately He will work it out for good.

Reflect on our standing in God's authority. This is a reflecting on the humility it takes to trust God's will and to yield to all that God desires even when it means cancer. Again this does not mean we rejoice in the cancer but we rejoice in the authority of God and the fact that He is greater than our cancer. That is what Peter means in the passage of Scripture found in 1 Peter 5:5-7 *"Likewise you younger people, submit yourselves to your elders. Yes, all of you be submissive to one another, and be clothed with humility, for "God resists the proud, But gives grace to the humble." Therefore humble yourselves under the mighty hand of God, that He may exalt you in due time, casting all your care upon Him, for He cares for you."* Peter found out firsthand that God resists the proud. After the resurrection Peter knew that he needed to humble himself under the mighty hand of God. He is sharing this with us so we will not be prideful but humble and yielded under God's hand for whatever He has in store for our lives.

When we understand God's love and His goodness we will yield to His authority knowing that He is over all things and will work all things out for good. Peter says cast your care, your cancer, on Him for He does indeed care for your cancer and all the cares that you have. The word for cast means just to lay it on Him and He will receive it. He will heal it. He will make it good as only the good God with all authority can do. There is no better place to be; whether we have cancer or we have a clean bill of health, than to be under God's love, goodness and authority over all things, even life and death.

Reflect on our standing in God's presence. Reflecting on God's presence means that we believe that He is loving, that He is good and that His authority is worth yielding to and that we can call on Him and He will hear us. In Isaiah 55:6, the Old Testament prophet Isaiah tells us, *"Seek the LORD while He may be found, Call upon Him while He is near."* We can seek the Lord; we can call on the Lord, for He is near and can be found. During our time of cancer let us reflect on the presence of God every day; seeking Him and calling on Him for our every need.

Reflecting on God's presence means seeking His kingdom as it tells us in Matthew 6:33 *"But seek first the kingdom of God and His righteousness, and all these things shall be added to you."* In seeking God during this time let us seek first His kingdom and righteousness and He will add to us all that we need. As we reflect on God's presence let us also seek to live here on this earth as we will in heaven. We find that truth also in Matthew 6:10 *"Your kingdom come. Your will be done on earth as it is in heaven."*

When we reflect on God's presence in this way, God will give to us the confidence and assurance that He has not left us and what He is allowing us to go through is good based on His goodness and love. Cancer allows us to know that this life and body is passing away. We will say as Paul did in 2 Corinthians 5:8 *"We are confident, yes, well pleased rather to be absent from the body and to be present with the Lord."* We pray for God to heal cancer and yet we are confident that if He does not when we are absent from this body, we will be present with the Lord in heaven. God's love is revealed in the words of Jesus in John 14:2-3 *"In My Father's house are many mansions; if it were not so, I would have told you. I go to prepare a place for you. And if I go and prepare a place for you, I will come again and receive you to Myself; that where I am, there you may be also."* God so loved us that He sent Jesus Christ to die for our sin. Jesus promises to come for us to take us to where He is, and where He is, is in heaven with His father, and they both desire for us to be with them forever. We need to reflect on God's love, His goodness, His authority and His presence as that which we desire above all things on this earth.

Life is short, painful, with uncertain outcomes and yet God is always available. We call on Him and seek Him for He is the only good God full of love and goodness with all authority to accomplish everything in our lives. He can heal our cancer and He can give us confidence through our cancer that no matter what happens to us on this earth He will not leave us or forsake us. He is preparing a place for us that where He is we may be forever.

Chapter Six

Why Cancer is a Way of Transformation

We have discovered that while we were yet sinners Christ died for us and that through His death we are saved. Through this salvation all condemnation has been removed and yet the apostle Paul says we still struggle with our old nature and our new nature. God is in the business of transforming our old nature to the new nature through a process called sanctification, making us His forever children. He is in the business of making us fit for our time in heaven.

One of the transformations that God makes in our life is to allow us to know that heaven is worth seeking. Paul said that he was given a thorn in the flesh so he would know that God was enough and His grace sufficient. Paul expressed that thought in 2 Corinthians 12:7 *"And lest I should be exalted above measure by the abundance of the revelations, a thorn in the flesh was given to me, a messenger of Satan to buffet me, lest I be exalted above measure."* If we never got sick, if cancer was never part of our lives, we may never desire heaven but only seek to live here on this earth. God wants us to seek heaven.

The apostle Paul tells us we have a part in Romans 12:1-2 *"I beseech you therefore, brethren, by the mercies of God, that you present your bodies a living sacrifice, holy, acceptable to God, which is your reasonable service. And do not be conformed to this world, but be transformed by the renewing of your mind, that you may prove what is that good and acceptable and perfect will of God."* We are to present our bodies, cancer free or full of cancer, under the almighty hand of God as we yield to His goodness and love. We are not to be conformed to this world, or love this world, but be transformed by the renewing of our mind to love God, the things of God and seek the kingdom of heaven. The Lord desires for us to seek His kingdom and His presence with the longing for heaven. Cancer is a means by which we can do so.

God desires for us to be like His dear son the Lord Jesus Christ. 2 Corinthians 3:18 states *"But we all, with unveiled face, beholding as in a mirror the glory of the Lord, are being transformed into the same image from glory to glory, just as by the Spirit of the Lord."* This is why we need to spend time in the word of God studying His word. The Word of God reveals to us the life of Jesus the one to whom we should emulate and be transformed into His likeness.

A wonderful truth the apostle Paul shares with us about this transformation is found in Philippians 1:6 *"being confident of this very thing, that He who has begun a good work in you will complete it until the day of Jesus Christ."* God indeed is active in and longing for our transformation, as we labor, as we yield, as we renew our minds by the word of the living God. God makes a promise to us that the good work that He started, while we were yet sinners, He will complete. He will make us complete in Christ Jesus our Lord.

This transformation is a longing in our hearts not just to know about the Lord Jesus Christ and God the Father but to truly know them. To be moved in our hearts to seek the kingdom of God not because we are told to but because we long for heaven. We long to be released from this body of disease and death, not only seeking a healthy body but one that is transformed by the glory of God to a purity of heart that will allow us to see God, to love God, and to be like our Savior Jesus Christ. Cancer is one of the means that God gives to some of us to transform us from seeking this world, the pleasures of this world and the comfort of this world to seeking Him.

Chapter Seven

Why Cancer is an Opportunity for Evangelism

This chapter title refers to the question and answer of why did we get cancer? It is a way God intends to use to draw us to Himself and to use us to draw others to God. We who know the Lord and have cancer must seek to live and allow our cancer to be a means for the lost to see the grace and love of God in us.

The Bible is clear when it speaks about God's love that brings us to salvation. He so loved us He came and He so loved us that once we are saved He leaves us here that others may see the salvation of His grace and mercy in our lives. If we were saved simply to go to heaven He would take us directly to heaven after we were saved. Yet, we see that once God saves us He leaves us here so our lives might be a testimony of His great salvation that He desires to give to all who will believe.

When Jesus Christ came from heaven to earth to die on the cross for our sin, the world saw Him from the time that He was born in a manger to His adulthood. As a child the world saw His obedience to His earthly parents and saw His life lived faithfully before God. The world saw His obedience to the Father in His adulthood as He fulfilled the law and followed His Father's will all the way to death on a cross to bring salvation to lost humanity. The gospel of Mark in 15:39 tells us how Christ was recognized as the Son of God, *"So when the centurion, who stood opposite Him, saw that He cried out like this and breathed His last, he said, "Truly this Man was the Son of God!"*

Not only could people see the way Jesus lived and died, allowing them to see the love of God, they also heard the words of our Lord Jesus as He died. Luke 23:34 says, *"Then Jesus said, "Father, forgive them, for they do not know what they do." And they divided His garments and cast lots."* When Jesus died on the cross He was fulfilling the Father's will to seek and to save that which was lost and prayed from the cross for them to be forgiven and come to believe.

In the New Testament we see the godly saints followed the example of the Lord Jesus Christ when they came to die. We see the example of Stephen in Acts 7:59-60 *"And they stoned Stephen as he was calling on God and saying, "Lord Jesus, receive my spirit." Then he knelt down and cried out with a loud voice, "Lord, do not charge them with this sin." And when he had said this, he fell asleep."* Stephen was an early New Testament saint who loved the Lord Jesus Christ and lived for Him. When Stephen was brought before the religious leaders and preached the message of God's love and forgiveness they rejected that message and stoned him to death. We see in Stephen's life and in his death that he lived and died that others would come to know the grace and mercy of the Lord Jesus. Stephen prayed even when he was dying that the Lord would bring them to repentance and they would come to believe on Christ.

The Bible is clear that God so loved the world He sent His Son not to make us comfortable or to live forever here on this earth but that we would come to know who He is, come to believe on the Lord Jesus Christ and be saved, receiving everlasting life. Luke 19:10 says, *"for the Son of Man has come to seek and to save that which was lost."* Often in our lives we think Jesus has come just to make us comfortable, profitable, and healthy, to do our bidding or do for us what we ask Him to do. We see the reason He came was to seek and to save that which was lost. We must also seek to live to see God save those who are lost.

The Apostle Paul tells us in Philippians 1:22 *"But if I live on in the flesh, this will mean fruit from my labor; yet what I shall choose I cannot tell."* Paul is telling us his living was to see other people come to hear the gospel and believe and be saved. He so loved and longed for the Lord Jesus Christ that he said it was hard for him to choose between the two, going to heaven or remaining on this earth. But either way his living on in the flesh was to share the gospel of God's salvation.

In 1 Corinthians 5:5 Paul shares that no sin and no loving of this world is a substitute for the salvation that God wants to give to us. Jesus said on one occasion; what would be the profit if a man gained the whole world but lost his soul (Matthew 16:26)? Paul was saying the same thing that Jesus said. The most important thing is for us to believe on the Lord Jesus Christ and be saved.

The Bible states clearly that all have sinned and fall short of the glory of God. The wages of that sin is death but the gift of God is eternal life (Romans 3:23; 6:23). The gift of God's everlasting life comes by repentance and belief not because one is better than another. On one occasion Jesus was told by some religious people about a group of Galileans who were trying to show how righteous they were. The religious people stated how undeserving of God's grace and mercy these Galileans were. Jesus' response to them in

Luke 13:1-5 reveals to us the importance of repentance and belief. Jesus said two times in these five verses that they were not worse sinners than all other Galileans but everyone must also repent or likewise perish. Salvation is a need that all humanity has and we who have been saved are not more righteous. We were in the same place, in the same situation as all who are lost in sin. But God's grace has been revealed to us through the gospel and we've come to believe and God has saved us. We understand unless one repents they will likewise perish, so our heart's desire is the same as Christ's desire, to see others come to repentance and be saved.

If you've come to believe on the Lord Jesus Christ and God has saved you, allow your cancer to be a means by which people can see this salvation. Pray during this difficult time of your life as you encounter people wherever you may be that they may see God through your words, your actions and your concern for them. Pray that God will use you and not just in giving religious clichés. Pray that as God's grace, mercy and salvation has comforted you it will comfort them as well. Pray to live for Christ, pray to die for Christ and pray that God will use our lives that others would come to repentance and salvation in the grace of the Lord Jesus Christ.

Chapter Eight

Why Cancer is a Reminder to Live Each Day

Receiving news you have cancer or some other illness that may lead to your death causes us to focus on the bad news and not on the days the Lord has given to us. Processing the news is appropriate and must be done but remaining and focusing only on the bad news can cause us not to live each day for the glory of God. The Bible tells us in Psalm 90:12 *"So teach us to number our days, That we may gain a heart of wisdom."* It is important for us to learn to number our days so when we come to the realization that we don't have an unlimited number of days, but a limited number, it will not distress us. We want to number our days so we can gain a heart of wisdom and live each day appropriately for our God. The Bible tells us in Ecclesiastes 3:2 there is *"A time to be born, And a time to die."* We have kept the first appointment because we are alive and we will keep that second appointment because we will all die. But living today, let us live this day to the glory of God.

One of the greatest Old Testament examples of living each day for the Lord is found in the book of Job. Job was a righteous man and lived for the Lord, loved the Lord and yet one day Satan came before the Lord accusing the saints. God offered Job as one that even in suffering would remain faithful to Him. Satan not only attacked Job's family and possessions but Job's health. Job's wife even told him to curse God and die (Job 2:9). Job had such a life of suffering that people the world over refer to him as an example when others fall into great suffering.

Job made a major mistake in the suffering that God allowed in his life by focusing on that suffering. When Job focused on the suffering he could not understand why or what was happening to him and he even questioned the goodness of God. Job questioned God to the point that he said that his suffering would lead to his death. Job said that in Job 30:20-23 *"I cry out to You, but You do not answer me; I stand up, and You regard me. But You have become cruel to me; With the strength of Your hand You oppose me. You lift me up to the wind and cause me to ride on it; You spoil my success. For I know that You will bring me to death."* Job was wrong. This suffering would not lead to his death. The suffering that God allowed into his life did not kill him but allowed him to come to know the Lord loved him, would provide for him and would bring him through the suffering.

When Job finally refocused on the Lord and no longer on his suffering he was able to say that God was wonderful and that he now knew that God loved him. Job understood God was using this time to allow him to live each day for the glory of His God. Listen to what Job says in Job 42:3-6 *"You asked, 'Who is this who hides counsel without knowledge?' Therefore I have uttered what I did not understand, Things too wonderful for me, which I did not know. Listen, please, and let me speak; You said, 'I will question you, and you shall answer Me.' "I have heard of You by the hearing of the ear, But now my eye sees You. Therefore I abhor myself, And repent in dust and ashes."*

Indeed God desires for us not to focus on our cancer but to focus on Him. Do not see this as the last day but as a day we are alive and should live for God. The Bible tells us in Mark 13:32 *"But of that day and hour no one knows, not even the angels in heaven, nor the Son, but only the Father."* Revealing to us that only God knows the times. So when we get bad news or news of cancer and even when a doctor may give to us a time frame we must always remember all time frames are known only by God Almighty. Yes, we listen to doctors and we follow schedules and we take the necessary steps for our health. But let us not focus on our bad health or bad circumstances but focus on the goodness of God and live for this day. You have today and I have today and we can live this day rejoicing in the day God has given all to His glory.

As Jesus walked this earth facing the day He would go to the cross He lived each day for the glory of God. He tells us that truth in John 9:4 *"I must work the works of Him who sent Me while it is day; the night is coming when no one can work."* Let us work today in the light of this day for night is coming. We will die one day and we will no longer be able to live for the Lord here on this earth, but we do have today so let us live this day.

James, the half-brother of Jesus, tells us in James 4:13-14 *"Come now, you who say, "Today or tomorrow we will go to such and such a city, spend a year there, buy and sell, and make a profit"; whereas you do not know what will happen tomorrow. For what is your life? It is even a vapor that appears for a little time and then vanishes away."* Our days are numbered, our life is a vapor, and we do not know what the day holds, nor do those around us. Therefore, let us not allow our cancer or our doctor's timeframe or even our own timeframe keep us from living this day for God's glory.

"Therefore do not worry about tomorrow, for tomorrow will worry about its own things. Sufficient for the day is its own trouble" (Matthew 6:34). Don't worry about tomorrow. Don't even worry about today. Live for today knowing that God is good and gracious and will provide all our needs according to His riches in glory (Philippines 4:19). We can trust Him and believe Him and live for Him this very day.

Let us proclaim as the psalmist did in Psalm 118:24 *"This is the day the LORD has made; We will rejoice and be glad in it."* Indeed this is the day the Lord has made for you and for me, let us rejoice and be glad in it, living for the glory of the Lord.

Chapter Nine

Why Cancer is Seeing God as Good

It is hard for us to imagine when we hear the news of cancer or any other bad news how it could be the best of all things. We know the Bible tells us that God is good and everything that He does is good so we know anything He allows in our life is good.

James tells us in James 1:17 *"Every good gift and every perfect gift is from above, and comes down from the Father of lights, with whom there is no variation or shadow of turning."* James tells us that every gift we get from God is good and comes down from the Lord God where there is no variation or shadow of turning. God does not change, He is always good. God is good each day of our lives; the days before we received the news of cancer and even the days after we received the news of cancer. Without variation, there's no changing, God will never cheat us nor let us down, He is good today and He will remain good forever.

Looking again at Romans 8:28 *"And we know that all things work together for good to those who love God, to those who are the called according to His purpose."* We know that all things work for good. This does not say what happens to us is good. For cancer is not good. But all things work out for good for we know God is good and gracious and will bring to pass that which is good for us.

That is the truth that we find in Philippians 1:6 *"being confident of this very thing, that He who has begun a good work in you will complete it until the day of Jesus Christ."* Life is hard and it seems to get more difficult when we receive the news of cancer or some other illness, but we are confident that that which Christ started will be completed. We know that through all the days of our lives God works everything out for the best even the completion of our days.

Jesus tells us in John 14:1-6 *"Let not your heart be troubled; you believe in God, believe also in Me. "In My Father's house are many mansions; if it were not so, I would have told you. I go to prepare a place for you." And if I go and prepare a place for you, I will come again and receive you to Myself; that where I am, there you may be also. "And where I go you know, and the way you know." Thomas said to Him, "Lord, we do not know where You are going, and how can we know the way?" Jesus said to him, "I am the way, the truth, and the life. No one comes to the Father except through Me."* The Bible tells us that God gave us His son that if we would believe on Him we would not perish but have everlasting life and in this passage we see this everlasting life. Jesus says that I love you, I will save you, I will not leave you or forsake you. I will provide for you throughout all the days of your life, and I am preparing a place and I will come for you. What great love God loved us with that He saved us, He will come for us and we will live with Him forever.

Having received the news of cancer I do not always feel good each day. Sometimes my mind wanders and I focus on the bad news. Yet I know because of God's word, the promise of Jesus to save me, and the promise we have in John 14:1-6 that He is coming for me, that I will be with Him forever and this is the best that can possibly happen to those of us who are in Christ Jesus.

Conclusion

Where am I today?

As I am writing this I am in a five to six week waiting period. I am waiting to have a follow up CT scan. I have gone through eight cycles of chemotherapy and six weeks of radiation and chemo. The process of which I find myself is as dictated by the cancer team at MUSC of Charleston. We are praying that the scan will show that the tumor has shrunk and I will be able to have surgery to remove the tumor. We trust the Lord and pray that indeed this will occur and surgery will be as soon as possible which is the only way the tumor can be removed.

I find myself today with the peace and comfort of the Lord Jesus Christ as promised in the Bible. During this period of time I am focusing on God and His Word and trusting in His promises to me of goodness and never leaving or forsaking me. I find in my heart the reality that God is good even as the psalmist said in Psalm 34:8 *"Oh, taste and see that the LORD is good; Blessed is the man who trusts in Him!"* During this time of my life I've tasted and truly see God is good and I will continue to trust in Him. I have also discovered what the psalmist expressed in Psalm 106:1

"Oh, give thanks to the LORD, for He is good! For His mercy endures forever."

As I pray and trust the Lord during this time I realize there are three possibilities. First, is the possibility the tumor will shrink, the surgery will remove the tumor and I will be healed going on in-service to the Lord Jesus Christ. Second, the tumor will not shrink and I will have to live with it a certain amount of time in God's grace living and serving Him each day for His glory. And third, in time the tumor will take my life and I will be translated into the very presence of my Lord Jesus Christ, who promised He will be with me and has prepared a place for me and will come and take me to be with Him.

In a way these are the options that everyone has before them even if they have not received the news of cancer. First, we need to recognize that we are going to die and with this recognition turn to the Lord Jesus Christ and be saved and serve Him each day of our life. Second, we need to recognize that we live with this sentence of death on us and will one day pass from this life and we need to trust the Lord Jesus Christ and be saved and serve Him each day of our life. And third, we will indeed die one day and we need to trust the Lord Jesus Christ and be saved to serve Him each day of our life until that day.

My prayer for you is no matter where you find yourself today please trust the Lord Jesus Christ and be saved and serve Him each day of your life.

If this life and this world in which we live is so great and wonderful and it is. If we love its beauty, its comforts, its joys, and its pleasures how great must God's heaven indeed be. The Bible tells us that *"eye has not seen nor ear heard what God has in store for those who love him"* (1 Corinthians 2:9). If God has been so good to us here and He has; if He has provided for us here and He has; and if He watches out for us and He does; how great will it be in heaven when we are with Him. It is beyond understanding and yet this is what is promised to all those who are in Christ Jesus.

In the book of Revelation 22:20 John says *"He who testifies to these things says, "Surely I am coming quickly." Amen. Even so, come, Lord Jesus!"* John is looking forward to the coming of the Lord Jesus Christ which should be every believer's heart's desire. Not because it is a bad day, or bad things have happened, or even because we have cancer. But because we long for, and desire the Lord Jesus Christ with all of our heart, our soul and our strength; may we so desire this and pray each day, "Even so come Lord Jesus!"

I would like to leave you with a poem written by William Cowper, a godly man who suffered much on this earth, yet never stopped believing in the goodness of God's love.

"God Moves in a Mysterious Way" by William Cowper

God moves in a mysterious way
His wonders to perform;
He plants His footsteps in the sea
And rides upon the storm.

Deep in unfathomable mines
Of never failing skill
He treasures up His bright designs
And works His sovereign will.

Ye fearful saints, fresh courage take;
The clouds ye so much dread

Are big with mercy and shall break
In blessings on your head.

Judge not the Lord by feeble sense,
But trust Him for His grace;
Behind a frowning providence
He hides a smiling face.

His purposes will ripen fast,
Unfolding every hour;
The bud may have a bitter taste,
But sweet will be the flower.

Blind unbelief is sure to err
And scan His work in vain;
God is His own interpreter,
And He will make it plain.

Cowper, William, (26 November 1731 - 24 April 1800) *God Moves in a Mysterious Way*, retrieved from http://www.poemhunter.com/god-moves-in-a-myterious-way (6-June-2012).

Printed in the United States
By Bookmasters